Mammalogy

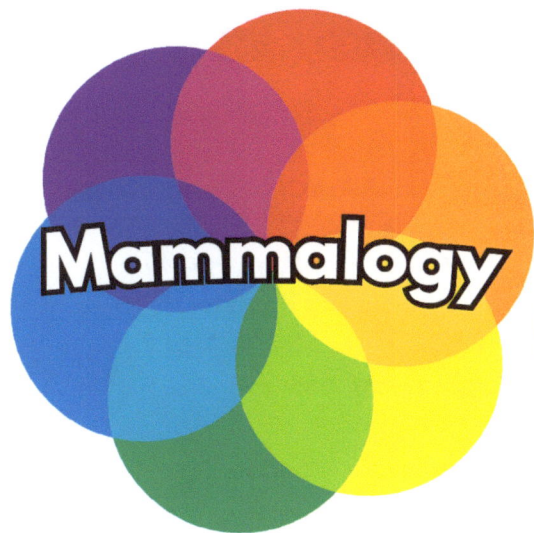

Book of COLORS
A Rainbow of Mammals

AO PRESS

Jessica Lee Anderson

Paperback ISBN: 978-1-964078-46-5

To Dawn Bartlett, thanks for your support and having a heart for animals of all kinds; and to Rowan, keep learning about animals and treasure memories with your precious Allie always. - JLA

Mammals are often multi-colored, so have fun pointing out the variety of colors in addition to the featured colors! Photos are not to scale.

Photo credits, left to right, top to bottom: Front cover: Own Garden (Mandrill); Interior cover: cynoclub (Rabbits); Dedication page: Life On White; p. 4: Freder, Timon Cornelisse, Cede Prudente; p. 5: Flickr, skhoward, webguzs; p. 6: Alexandra Draghici, Anolis01, Ondrej Prosicky; p. 7: StockSnap, CCaetano, Mátyás Varga; p. 8: Sharon Snider, Nemyrivskyi Viacheslav, Danielrao; p. 9: Hedrus, BirdImages, zwawol; p. 10: invertedatlas, Nachosuch, Ken Canning; p. 11: Vadim B, Freder, richcarey; p. 12: ixus142, gsagi, Rixipix; p. 13: Digital Vision, Michel Viard, Amanda Lewis; p. 14: Roger Brown, Katherine Davis, siempreverde22; p. 15: Peak Mystique, Rocter, USO; p. 16: Hunted Duck, Hemera Technologies, Nicholas Dale; p. 17: Jillian Cooper, Lingbeek, TakinPix; p. 18: eddy.galeotti, rainngirl, Ahmed Sobhy; p. 19: Mikhail Semenov, Dmitry Bogdanov, designerpoint; p. 20: Hillebrand Breuker, CarbonBrain, Fenlanddavid; p. 21: Mantaphoto, micheldenijs, Wayne Jackson; p. 22: rick734's Images, Tanukiphoto, dlanier; p. 23: Lev Tsimbler, Luis Jimenez Benito, outcast85; p. 24: Andyworks, Jupiterimges, Travelnshot; p. 25: Jason Prince, MaZiKab, Kaylan Chavers; p. 26: Life On White, Chingkai Huang, MundoCurioso23; p. 27: Emily Trupiano, htrnr, chendongshan; p. 28: CraigRJD, Michel Viard, Andrew Haysom; p. 29: pixelshot, Ju Photographer, Zuzule; 30: mikiange, Aktarul Islam, Ivkovich; p. 31: Pixel-mixer, javarman3, Charoenchai Tothaisong; p. 32: Anolis01, voraorn, Zuzule; p. 33: Saddako, Freder, Pascale Gueret; p. 34: Michael Anderson; Back cover: Life On White (Cheetah)

This Book Belongs to:

_____

Mammalogy is the study of mammals like cats, dogs, dolphins, primates, and more.

Lion

Red

Orangutan mother and baby

Western red colobus monkeys

Red pigment is usually less common in mammals compared to other classes of animals like amphibians or fish.

Red giant flying squirrel

Red

Red panda

Mammals are "warm-blooded"— their body temperature will stay steady and warm even if it is cold outside.

Red angus cow

Red howler monkey

Orange

Persian cat

Golden lion tamarin

Mammals live in a wide range of environments and can be found all around the world.

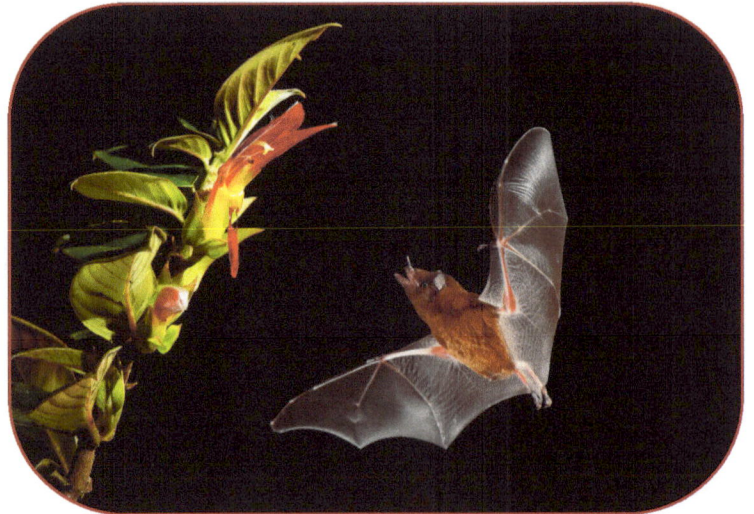

Orange nectar bat

Orange

Red fox

The majority of mammals on Earth are livestock and pets rather than wild animals.

Tiger

Shiba Inu

Yellow

Yellow Labrador retriever

Palomino horse

Mammals are vertebrates, meaning they have a backbone (vertebral column).

Gee's golden langur

Yellow

Yellow baboons

Mammal mothers have mammary glands that produce milk to nourish their babies.

Yellow-bellied marmot

Yellow mongoose

Green

Three-toed sloth

Three-toed sloth

There are no mammals with green pigments, though sloths often appear green due to algae that grows on their fur.

Three-toed sloth mother and baby

Blue

Russian blue kitten

Mandrill

Blue whale

Only a few mammal species have blue features or are blue-gray in color.

Purple

Poodle puppy

Great Danes

Genetic traits, pigment, and lighting can cause some mammals to look purple. Hippos secrete an oily red fluid which can give them a purple hue.

Hippopotamus mother and baby

Pink

Yorkshire pig

Certain mammals may be born pink due to less pigment, although some species may become pinker as they age.

Pink river dolphin

Nine-banded armadillo

13

Black

Black water buffaloes

Black bear mother and babies

Hair or fur is something that sets mammals apart from other animals. Every mammal has hair or fur at some point in their lives.

Black panther

14

Black

Short-finned pilot whale

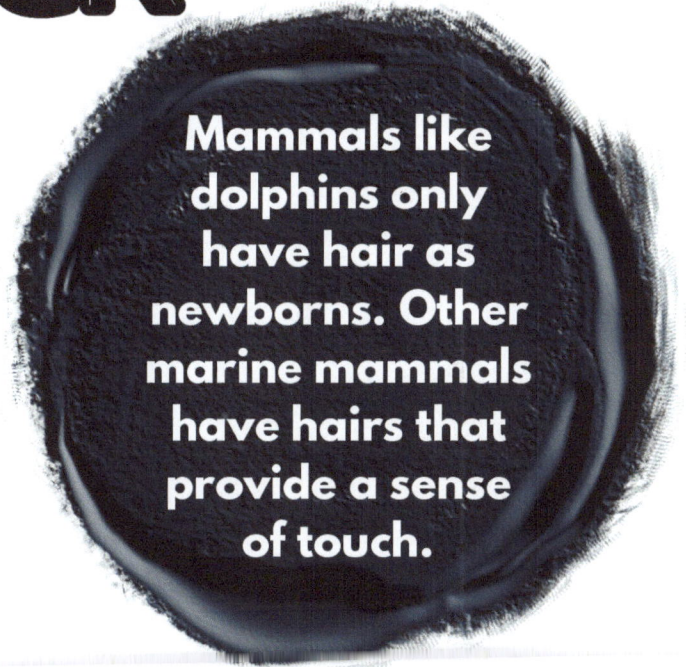

Mammals like dolphins only have hair as newborns. Other marine mammals have hairs that provide a sense of touch.

Celebes crested macaque

Bonobos

White

Polar bear

Artic harp seal

Certain mammals grow a thick fur coat when it becomes cold. Some species change from brown or gray in the summer to snow white in the winter.

Artic hare

White

Mountain goat

Fur and hair (including wool) keep mammals warm and protects them from rain.

Beluga whale

Merino sheep

Gray

Harbor seal

Gray whale

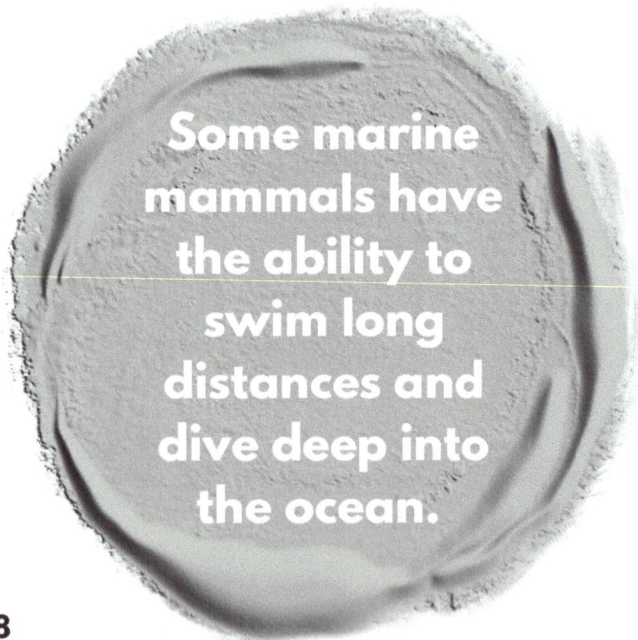

Some marine mammals have the ability to swim long distances and dive deep into the ocean.

Bottlenose dolphins

Gray

Many mammals protect and look after their babies until they are ready to live on their own.

Gray wolf

Common mole rat

African elephants

Brown

Capybara

American bison

Bats are the only mammal to freely fly. Many mammal species are capable of running.

Daubenton's bat

Brown

Brown bear mother and cubs

Mammals have complex brains! Scientists are learning more about mammal intelligence and social structures.

Walrus

Bactrian camel

COLOR Combinations

Can you describe the colors and patterns of these mammals?

Gray squirrel

Red-rumped agouti

Gray fox

COLOR Combinations

Squirrel monkey

Red-shanked douc langur

Yunnan black snub-nose monkey

How are the colors of these primates similar and different?

COLOR Combinations

What colors do these big cats have in common?

Snow leopard

Cheetah

Jaguar

COLOR Combinations

Giraffes

Hyena

Llama

What are some things you notice about the shapes, colors, and features of these mammals?

COLOR Combinations

What colors do you see? Why do you think these mammals have stripes?

Zebra

Okapi

Bongo

COLOR Combinations

Blue heeler

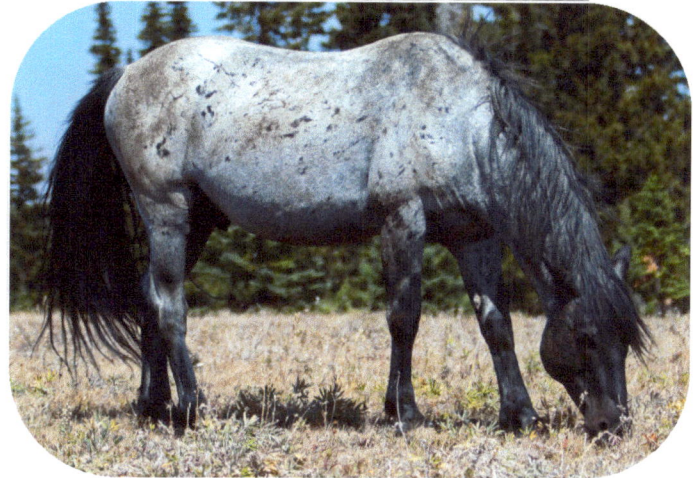
Blue roan stallion

British short hair cat

What do you notice about the colors of these mammals?

COLOR Combinations

What colors are these mammals? What are some other things you notice about them?

Tasmanian devil

Giant otter

Echidna

COLOR Combinations

Can you describe the colors and patterns of these mammals?

Dalmatian dog

Holland lop rabbit

Appaloosa horse

COLOR Combinations

How do you think colors might help mammals in the wild?

Giant panda

Black and white ringtailed lemur

Orca

COLOR Combinations

Fruit bat

Aye-aye

Slow loris

What colors do these mammals have in common? What are some differences?

COLOR Combinations

Can you describe the colors and patterns of the mammals?

Blue-eyed lemurs

Siamese cat

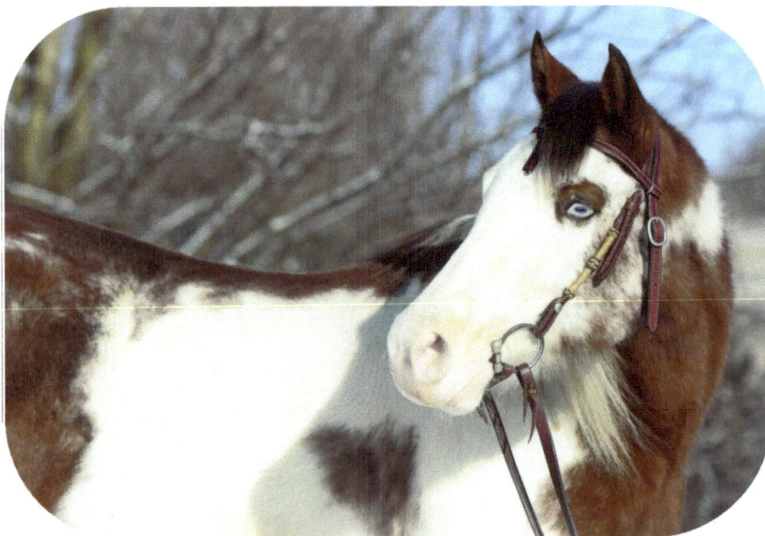
American paint horse

COLOR Combinations

Why do you think the colors, shapes, and features of a mammal matters?

African crested porcupine

European badger

Giant anteater

Jessica Lee Anderson is an award-winning author of over 75 books for young readers including the NAOMI NASH chapter book series. Jessica loves spending time in nature and exploring the outdoors with her husband, Michael, and their daughter, Ava! You can learn more about Jessica by visiting www.jessicaleeanderson.com.

Check out these other books:

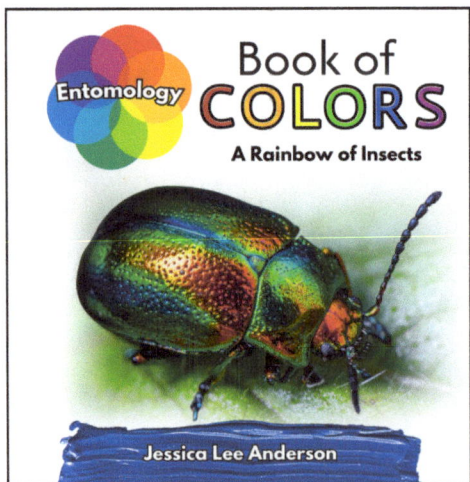

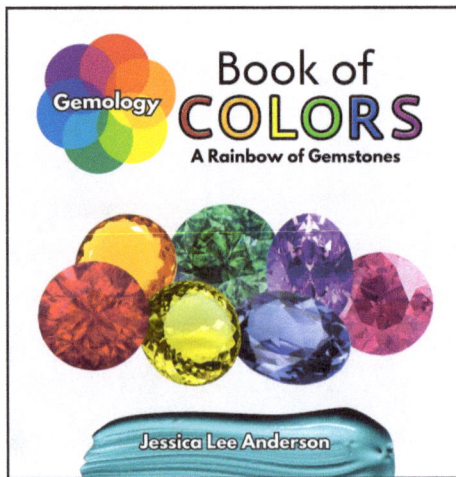

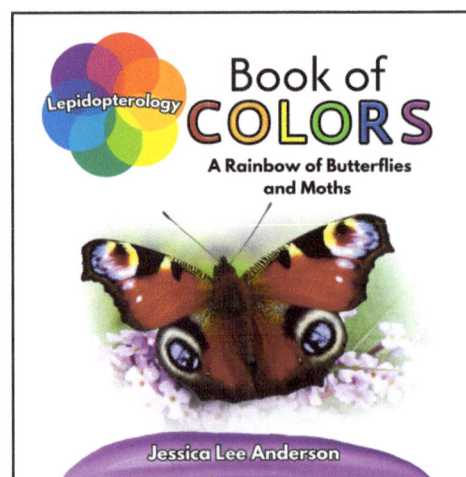

Entomology
Book of COLORS
A Rainbow of Insects
Jessica Lee Anderson

Gemology
Book of COLORS
A Rainbow of Gemstones
Jessica Lee Anderson

Lepidopterology
Book of COLORS
A Rainbow of Butterflies and Moths
Jessica Lee Anderson